Foreword

Trying to persuade my two young kids that eating fruit and vegetables will turn them into superheroes hasn't really worked! When I found myself agreeing to Archie dipping carrots in chocolate sauce, I knew something had to be done.

Star Cooks is compiled by Victoria Chilcott

So I set about contacting real superheroes: Jamie Oliver, Gordon Ramsay, Hugh Fearnley-Whittingstall, Delia Smith, and all the brilliant world-class chefs who have contributed to this book. Now we have a great cook book for both kids and parents to try out fun and healthy food together. Hooray!

But *Star Cooks* is much more than a fun way for kids to learn about food. It helps raise funds and awareness for the food charity FareShare. The volunteers work tirelessly to redistribute food to vulnerable people who need to eat. By buying this book, you will help FareShare continue its great work and, hopefully, you and your kids will have fun cooking these wonderful recipes. Enjoy!

Victoria Chilcott

About FareShare...

What happens to:
- ★ food that doesn't sell at the supermarket?
- ★ unsold sandwiches from sandwich shops?
- ★ apples from the market that have gone uneaten?
- ★ even an airline's unused, unopened bottles of water?

The food is all within its sell-by-date and lots of it is really healthy and yummy too. And there are TONS of it that would go to waste every day if it wasn't for FareShare.

Food that would often end up in landfill sites, littering up the country, is instead taken in a FareShare van, by FareShare volunteers, and given to people who need it.

Some of the people who get great food from FareShare are homeless people in shelters, disadvantaged children in breakfast clubs, elderly people in day centres, and vulnerable people who have been socially excluded.

Good food makes you feel better, healthier, and more confident. It makes all the difference to a vulnerable person who is seeking help to solve their problems, and improve their life.

collect the food

load the vans

share it out

FareShare
community food network

star tips

Look out for cooking tips from the chefs.

When you see this sign it means that you need an adult to give you a hand.

warning sign

Cleaning up is part of cooking! So help with the washing up or stacking the dishwasher.

Number of servings

you will need

cooking time

These symbols give you information on things you need, how much time a recipe takes, and how many people it serves.

adult help

kitchen kit

It's a good idea to read through each recipe and measure out the

Kitchen rules OK

All the chefs in this book have clean and safe kitchens. So follow the Star Cooks' kitchen rules for fun, safe, and successful cooking.

Make all your tbsp (tablespoon) and tsp (teaspoon) measures level.

Be clean

1 wash hands
Always wash your hands before and after cooking.

2 wash fruit and veg
Wash all fruit and vegetables before cooking them.

3 wash up
Wash up as you go along, and keep work surfaces clear.

4 Chopping board
Use separate chopping boards for meat and vegetables or fruit, or wash chopping boards between use.

5 Cover up
Wear an apron or old shirt to keep your clothes clean.

Be Safe

1 Ask a grown-up
Get an adult to help when cutting, blending, using the oven or hob, and any other electrical equipment.

2 It's hot
Keep your hands away from boiling kettles and hot pans. Remember, steam can burn too.

3 It's Sharp
Keep fingers well away when you're slicing, or grating. And never walk around with a knife.

4 It's electric
Dry your hands before using electrical items and unplug them when you have finished.

5 Pan handles
Turn saucepan handles to the side so the pans won't get knocked over.

Be Sensible

1 Chop on a board
Chop food on a chopping board, not the work surface.

2 Heat-proof
Put hot dishes onto heat-proof mats.

3 Tie back
Roll up long, loose sleeves and tie back long hair.

4 Sweep up
Sweep the floor when you've finished, or if you drop something, so you don't slip on it.

5 Have fun...
...but concentrate.

Food labels

Reading food labels and healthy eating go hand-in-hand. They tell you what's in the food you're buying.

Label for a 150g pot of fruit yoghurt

NUTRITION INFORMATION

Typical Values	per 100g	per pot
Energy Values	233kJ	352kJ
	55kcal	83kcal
Protein	4.0g	6.0g
Carbohydrate	7.3g	11g
of which sugars	6.6g	9.9g
Fat	1.1g	1.7g
of which saturates	0.7g	1.1g
Fibre	0.6g	0.9g
Sodium	0.1g	0.2g

Figuring it out

Your body needs the right mix of nutrients to stay healthy. The guideline daily amounts for kids aged 5–10 are in brackets.

Energy values (1800 kcal): this tells you how many calories (energy) a food contains.

Protein (65g): protein helps you grow and builds up your muscles to make you strong.

Carbohydrate (220g): this gives you energy. **Sugar** is a form of carbohydrate.

Fat (70g): your body needs fat to make cells. It stores fat to use for energy later. There are two types of fat, saturated and unsaturated. Unsaturated is healthier than saturated fat.

Fibre (24g): this helps food pass through your body and keeps your digestive system healthy.

Sodium (4g): this is another word for salt.

8

Good food guide

Knowing what foods are healthy is important for budding chefs. Take a look at this menu and the new food guide pyramid to help you plan your meals.

A healthy day

Enjoy the day the *Star Cooks* way! Food that you make yourself need have no hidden ingredients, like E numbers or preservatives, and is more fun to cook and tastier to eat.

☆ ☆☆ **MENU** ☆ ☆
breakfast
Eggy bread
What a smoothie!

— ☆ ☆☆ —

lunch
Red pepper and chickpea
hummus
Tandoori phal

☆ ☆☆

snack
crunchy apple cake bars

— ☆ ☆☆☆ —

tea
Smoked haddock and salmon
fishcakes with peas
Quaking pudding

Start right with these two recipes – bread for those energy-giving carbohydrates (carbs), egg for protein, and a fruit smoothie for a filling vitamin boost.

Hummus, with crunchy veg and pitta strips for dipping, is full of goodness. Fruity Tandoori phal will add to your 5-a-day.

This tasty snack has fibre and carbs to keep you going.

A healthy fish dish with peas and a calcium-rich pudding make a great main meal to end the day.

Pyramid power!

Ready, teady, go!

Exercise and drinking lots of water are important too.

The coloured stripes on the pyramid represent the five food groups, plus fats and oils, in the right proportions for a balanced diet. Eat food from every colour, every day.

Grains

Make it wholegrain

Bread and cereals make up the grain group. This is the biggest group and the foods in it will give you loads of energy.

Eat wholegrain bread, rice, cereals, or pasta.

Eat 6 servings per day.
1 serving is:
★ a slice of bread
★ a bowl of muesli
★ a plateful of rice or pasta

Vegetables

Vary your veggies

Vegetables are full of essential vitamins and minerals, fibre, and other disease-preventing goodness.

Eat 3-5 servings per day.
1 serving is:
★ 2 medium carrots
★ 3 broccoli florets
★ a small glass of vegetable juice

Fruits

Nature's treats

Fruits are as good for you as vegetables. Fresh, frozen, tinned, or dried – they're all good.

So make sure you eat 2-4 servings per day.
1 serving is:
★ a piece of fruit
★ a handful of dried fruit
★ a bowl of tinned fruit
★ a small glass of fruit juice

fats and oils

Nuts, vegetable oil, and fish are the best source.

milk products

Get your calcium-rich foods

Cheese, ice cream, and yoghurt are full of calcium which is good for your bones.

Eat 3 servings per day.
1 serving is:
★ a glass of milk
★ a pot of yoghurt
★ 2 slices of cheese

meat & beans

Protein

Meat, fish, beans, peas, eggs, nuts, and seeds contain protein.

2 servings per day.
1 serving is:
★ 1 chicken breast
★ a pile of beans or peas
★ a small bag of nuts or seeds

9

5 a day...
the colour way

leeks

green

Not only do green fruit and vegetables look and taste wonderful, they also help you stay sharp-eyed, strong-boned – and they keep your teeth tough too.

broccoli

green apple

celery

orange and yellow

Go for gold with sunny yellow and orange fruit and veg. They are full of vitamins and help you fight off colds.

nectarine

peach

mango

lemon

sweetcorn

white

White, tan, and brown fruit and vegetables help keep your heart healthy and strong. So go bananas!

ginger

onion

cauliflower

red

Stay raring to go with delicious red apples, cherries, raspberries, strawberries, rhubarb, and tomatoes. They'll help your memory, too!

red pepper

cherries

red onion

blue and purple

Add shades of blue and purple to your plate, and make your body strong and healthy with the fibre, vitamins, and minerals in these fruit and vegetables.

plum

blueberries

grapes

raisins

  Eat your greens! And your oranges, reds, yellows,

Eating 5–9 portions of fruit and vegetables every day helps you feel great. And eating a mixture of different coloured fruit and veg means you best use all their super powers.

lettuce
asparagus
kiwi fruit
pear
grapes
cabbage
lime
green beans

pumpkin
grapefruit
carrots
squash
orange
pineapple

parsnip
fennel
garlic
potatoes
banana
shallot
mushrooms

watermelon
red apple
strawberries
rhubarb
tomato
radish
raspberries

blackberries
blackcurrants
red cabbage
figs
aubergine

and blues! The more colourful the better...

Rise and Shine, it's...

breakfast ...time

John Burton Race ★ Hugh Fearnley-whittingstall

Did you know that
breakfast is the most important
meal of the day? Your body and brain need
fuel to think, walk, talk, and anything else you
do. Eating breakfast improves concentration, helps
your memory, and improves your mood. Good foods
to eat for breakfast are bread and muffins because
they are full of energy-giving carbohydrates. Fruit
gives you fibre and a burst of vitamins, and the
protein in eggs helps to build you up
for the day ahead.

Gordon Ramsay

All Set?
Let's go!

If you've got an egg, you've got a meal. Boil it, scramble it, flip it in hot oil, or crack it into gently boiling water and poach it – an egg is a different breakfast or supper for every day of the week.

Boiled egg

Hugh Fearnley-Whittingstall

timing

Cooking:
4½ minutes

serves 1

what you need

1 large egg
1 slice of thick-cut bread
butter
salt and pepper

kitchen kit

small saucepan
large spoon
timer
eggcup

1 Add water to a saucepan until three-quarters full and set it on the hob to boil. When the water starts to bubble, place the egg on a spoon and gently lower it into the water, using the side of the saucepan to ease the egg in. Immediately switch the timer on to 4½ minutes.

2 Toast the bread in a toaster then spread it with butter. Cut the toast into soldiers (strips) to serve with the egg.

3 When the timer finishes, taking great care, scoop the egg out of the boiling water with the spoon. Stand the egg in the eggcup.

4 Bash the top of the egg and slice it off with a spoon, sprinkle with a little salt and pepper if you like, and eat with a teaspoon and the toast soldiers.

Hugh Fearnley-Whittingstall

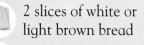

Serves 2

Preparation: 5 minutes
Cooking: 4 minutes

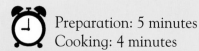

what you need

2 slices of white or
light brown bread

2 free-range eggs

salt and black pepper

1 tbsp sunflower
or olive oil

kitchen kit

knife

bread board

bowl

fork

frying pan

fish slice

How to do it...

1

Cut the bread into fat
fingers – two or three
of your fingers wide.

2

Break the eggs into the bowl.
Add a pinch of salt and a
grinding of pepper and beat
well until the yolks and whites
have frothed up together.

3

Drop as many bread fingers into the
eggy mixture as you can fit, turning
them over so that the egg sticks to
the bread on both sides. Let them sit
in the bowl for a couple of minutes so
that the egg really soaks into them.

4

Put the frying pan on the hob, pour in
the oil and switch on to medium heat.
When the oil is hot, place the bread
fingers in the pan. The egg will bubble
up and sizzle nicely in the hot oil.

5

After about a minute, the fingers will
be golden brown underneath, so flip
them over with the fish slice and cook
the other side. When they're done, lift
them out and put them on a warm
plate while you cook the rest.

Eggy bread

eggy

jammy

cheesy

egg with a tsp of sugar. Then spread your bread with jam.

Gordon Ramsay

 **Serves 4**

 Preparation: 10 minutes

 what you need

 400ml (14 fl oz) chilled natural yoghurt

 100ml (3½ fl oz) cold milk

 1 tsp honey

 1 small mango, peeled and roughly chopped

 150g (5oz) strawberries, hulled

 1 tbsp icing sugar

 kitchen kit

 blender

 teaspoon

 glasses

what a Smoooothie!

It is really important to get into the habit of eating fruit and vegetables. My four young and adorable kids at home, who all like different food, love this smoothie...

... My wife, Tana, and I love it too!

Gordon Ramsay.

18

This Smoothie is a great way to get lots of healthy vitamins and calcium – in one delicious drink.

mango

Strawberry

How to do it...

1 Pour half the yoghurt and milk into a blender. Add a tsp of honey and the chopped mango.

2 Whizz until smooth and divide between four glasses.

3 Repeat with the remaining yoghurt, milk, strawberries, and icing sugar. Blend until smooth.

4 Slowly pour the strawberry smoothie over the mango smoothie. You end up with layers of light yellow and pink.

John Burton Race

Blueberry muffins

These muffins are a family favourite – in particular with my wife Kim. They are delicious when still warm from the oven.

makes 16

Preparation: 15 minutes
Cooking: 20 minutes

what you need

 butter for greasing

 500g (1lb 2oz) plain flour, plus extra for dusting

 1 tbsp baking powder

 2 tsp custard powder

 250g (8oz) caster sugar

 185g (6½oz) fresh blueberries

 2 eggs

 185ml (6½ fl oz) milk

 185ml (6½ fl oz) sunflower oil

 icing sugar for dusting

kitchen kit

 muffin tin   sieve

 2 large bowls   whisk

 wooden spoon

Serve dusted with icing sugar.

20

How to do it...

1 Preheat the oven to 190°C/375°F/gas 5. Grease a muffin tin with butter and dust with flour, shaking out any excess flour.

2 Sift the flour, baking powder, and custard powder into a large bowl. Add the sugar, then the blueberries.

3 In a separate bowl, mix together the eggs, milk, and sunflower oil.

4 Make a well in the dry ingredients, add the milk mixture and combine, taking care not to over mix.

5 Spoon the batter into the prepared muffin tins and bake in the oven for 20 minutes or until golden and springy to the touch.

Main Meals and

Jean-Christophe Novelli ★ Antony Worrall Thompson
Antonio Carluccio ★ Jamie Oliver ★ Keith Floyd
Annabel Karmel ★ Nick Nairn ★ Tom Aikens ★ Ken Hom

A main meal should
have a mixture of protein,
carbohydrate, and lots of veggies! Most
people eat one main meal every day. In this
section there are lots of delicious dishes. You
can practise your kneading skills making
focaccia and pizza bases, cook up a
10 minute stir-fry, or choose one
of the succulent pies.

light bites

* Ruth Rogers and Rose Gray
* Marcus Wareing
* Lesley Waters
* Prue Leith

Let's do **lunch**

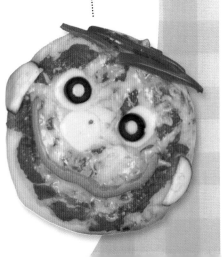

23

Nick Nairn

 serves 6

 Preparation: 10 minutes
Cooking: 50 minutes

 what you need

 750g (1½lb) fresh
butternut squash

 3 unpeeled garlic cloves

 4 tbsp olive oil

 2 medium onions,
finely sliced

 2 celery sticks, chopped

 60g (2oz) long grain rice

 1½ l (2½ pt)
vegetable or chicken stock

 salt and pepper

 4 tbsp chopped
fresh parsley

 kitchen kit

 knife and spoon

 roasting pan

large saucepan

 blender

24

Roasted butternut squash Soup

Even if you're not too keen on vegetables, this bright orange, subtly sweet and silky soup will win you over.

Happy Cooking!
Nick Nairn x

How to do it...

 **1** Preheat the oven to 200°C/400°F/ gas 6. Cut the squash in half and scrape out the seeds. Ask a grown-up to help with the squash.

 **2** Cut off the skin and cut the flesh into large cubes. Place the cubes in a roasting pan with the garlic cloves.

 **3** Toss the garlic and squash with 2 tbsp olive oil and then pop them in the oven to roast for about 30 minutes.

 **4** Heat the rest of the olive oil in a large saucepan and add the onions and celery. Cook over a gentle heat for 10 minutes until beginning to brown and soften.

 **5** Now stir in the rice, pour in the stock, and bring the mix to the boil. Cover and simmer for 15 minutes or until the rice is tender.

 **6** Remove the squash and garlic from the oven. Leave them until cool enough to handle, then pop the garlic cloves out of their skins.

 **7** Add the garlic and squash to the saucepan, bring to the boil, and simmer for 10 minutes. Liquidise or roughly blend the soup and return it to the pan.

 **8** Taste and season with salt and plenty of freshly ground black pepper. Add extra stock or water if the soup seems too thick. Sprinkle with parsley before serving.

Star tip Try toasting slices of bread and cutting them into shapes with a pastry cutter to go with your soup.

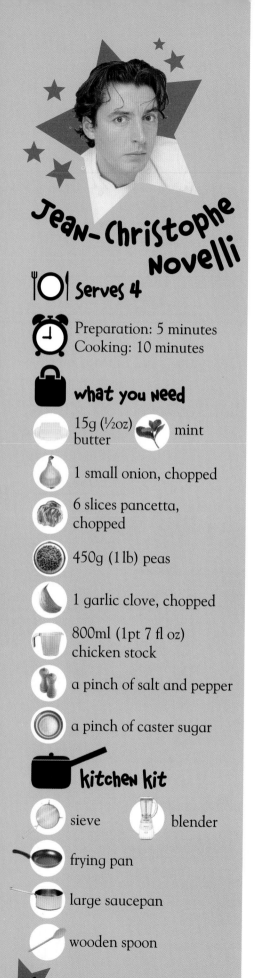

Jean-Christophe Novelli

🍽 **Serves 4**

⏰ Preparation: 5 minutes
Cooking: 10 minutes

🔒 **what you need**

- 15g (½oz) butter
- mint
- 1 small onion, chopped
- 6 slices pancetta, chopped
- 450g (1 lb) peas
- 1 garlic clove, chopped
- 800ml (1pt 7 fl oz) chicken stock
- a pinch of salt and pepper
- a pinch of caster sugar

🍳 **kitchen kit**

- sieve
- blender
- frying pan
- large saucepan
- wooden spoon

How to do it...

1

Heat the butter in a large pan, add the onion, and cook gently until see-through.

2

Get a frying pan very hot, add the pancetta, and quickly fry until crisp.

3

Add the pancetta to the large pan, together with the peas and garlic, and cook for a few minutes.

4

Pour in the stock and bring to a simmer. Cook until the peas are soft to the touch. Add a sprig of mint, season, and then add the sugar.

5

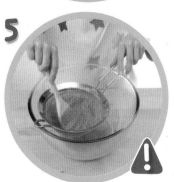

Whizz the mixture in a blender until smooth, then push through a fine sieve (or you can eat it up as it is if you want).

Pea Soup

with pancetta and mint

smoky bacon taste. It takes next-to-no-time to cook and is

combination and, o course, it is good for you too!

Lesley Waters

 Serves 6

 Preparation: 10 minutes
Cooking: 35–40 minutes

 for the chips

 900g (2lb) large
potatoes, scrubbed

 3 tbsp olive oil

 3 tbsp dark soy sauce

 black pepper

 for the dip

 125g (4oz) tinned
tuna, flaked

 1 tbsp mayonnaise

 200g (7oz) Greek yoghurt

 3 spring onions,
chopped

 kitchen kit

 knife

 roasting tin

large bowl

 wooden spoon

28

chips and dips

Everyone loves chips, and these chunky chips are easy to make and healthy too. Eat them with the tuna dip for a light lunch.

How to make the chips...

1 Preheat the oven to 200°C/400°F/gas 6. Cut the potatoes into very thick chips and place in a large, non-stick roasting tin.

2 Pour on the oil and soy sauce and toss together. Season with black pepper.

3 Bake in the oven for 35–40 minutes, turning occasionally, until golden brown and crisp.

How to make the dip...

1 In a bowl, mix together the tuna, mayonnaise, Greek yoghurt, and chopped spring onions.

2 Transfer the dip to a serving dish and chill in the fridge until you need it.

3 When the potatoes are out of the oven and cool enough to touch, dip in.

Star tip Dip your chips into salsa, guacamole, tzatziki, sour cream and chive, or anything you like. Great party food!

marcus

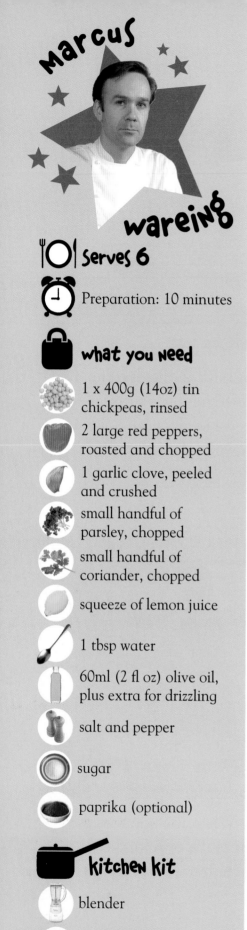

wareing

Serves 6

Preparation: 10 minutes

what you need

- 1 x 400g (14oz) tin chickpeas, rinsed
- 2 large red peppers, roasted and chopped
- 1 garlic clove, peeled and crushed
- small handful of parsley, chopped
- small handful of coriander, chopped
- squeeze of lemon juice
- 1 tbsp water
- 60ml (2 fl oz) olive oil, plus extra for drizzling
- salt and pepper
- sugar
- paprika (optional)

kitchen kit

- blender
- serving bowl

Red pepper and chickpea hummus

Hummus is easy and good for you too. I love the orangey-pink colour of this version.

How to do it...

1 Put the chickpeas, red peppers, garlic, parsley, coriander, lemon juice, and water into a blender and blend into a coarse paste.

2 Slowly trickle in the olive oil in a steady stream. Then whizz the paste a bit longer to make it smoother. Season to taste with salt, pepper – and a pinch of sugar.

3 Spoon into a serving bowl. Drizzle with a little more olive oil and sprinkle with paprika if you like.

with lots of crunchy snacks. Try breadsticks, raw vegetables

Then spend your lunch break dipping in.

pitta bread.

Annabel Karmel

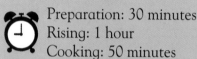 **Serves 4**

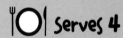 Preparation: 30 minutes
Rising: 1 hour
Cooking: 50 minutes

for the dough

225g (7½oz) strong white flour, plus extra for dusting

1 tsp fast action easy blend yeast

½ tsp salt

1 tsp sugar

2 tbsp olive oil, plus extra for oiling

150mla (5 fl oz) warm water

kitchen kit

2 large bowls

spoon

clingfilm

Three cheese funny face pizzas

I't's fun kneading and rolling out dough and it's easy to make your own delicious tomato sauce. Finish off by making faces on your pizzas using your favourite toppings.

Annabel Karmel

How to make the dough...

1 First oil a large bowl – use a piece of kitchen roll to spread the oil evenly.

2 Mix the flour, yeast, salt, and sugar together in another large bowl. Make a well in the middle and add the oil and water.

3 Mix the ingredients with a spoon, then your hands, to make a soft dough.

4 Turn out the dough onto a floured surface and knead for around 10 minutes until it is smooth and elastic.

5 To test whether the dough has been kneaded enough, poke a finger into the dough – if it springs back, it's ready.

6 Put the dough into the oiled bowl, cover, and leave in a warm place to rise for an hour or until almost doubled in size.

while the dough is rising, make the tomato sauce and prepare the toppings.

for the sauce

 1 tbsp extra virgin olive oil

 ½ medium red onion, chopped

 1 garlic clove, crushed

 1 x 400g (14oz) tin chopped tomatoes

 1 tbsp tomato puree

 2 tbsp dark brown sugar

 salt and pepper

 1 tbsp chopped basil

 the cheese

 60g (2oz) mozzarella, diced

 15g (½oz) Cheddar cheese, grated

 15g (½oz) Parmesan, grated

 kitchen kit

 large saucepan

 wooden spoon

knife

rolling pin

baking sheet

How to make the faces...

7 To make the tomato sauce, heat the oil and cook the onion for 5 or 6 minutes. Add the garlic and cook for another minute.

8 Stir in the chopped tomatoes, tomato puree, and sugar and season to taste. Cook, uncovered, for 30 minutes until thick. Stir in the basil.

9 Now test the risen dough by pressing it with your finger – it should leave a mark. Knead the dough for about a minute and then cut it into quarters.

10 Shape the quarters into balls and roll out on a floured surface using a rolling pin sprinkled with flour. Place the circles on a baking sheet.

11 Preheat the oven to 200°C/ 400°F/gas 6. Spread the tomato sauce on each pizza base. Sprinkle the cheese over the top.

12 Make faces using your favourite toppings, then cook in the oven for 12 minutes or until golden and bubbling.

 34

Make pepperoni ears, sweetcorn and olive eyes,

courgette hair, and big red pepper smiles.

funny

faces!

Anything goes.

They can be as silly as you like.

Ken Hom

 serves 4

 Preparation: 10 minutes
Cooking: 3–5 minutes

 what you need

 225g (7½oz) fresh peeled raw prawns

 1 tsp salt

 3 tsp sesame oil

 1½ tbsp vegetable oil

 1 tbsp chopped garlic

 1 tbsp chopped fresh ginger

 225g (7½oz) frozen peas, thawed

 2 tbsp chopped spring onions

2 tbsp water

 **kitchen kit**

 small bowl

 wok

 wooden spoon

 36

Prawn and pea Stir fry

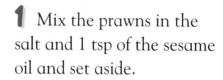

How to do it...

1 Mix the prawns in the salt and 1 tsp of the sesame oil and set aside.

2 Heat a wok or large frying pan until it is hot. Then add the vegetable oil. Pop the garlic, ginger, and prawns into the wok and stir-fry for roughly 30 seconds. Watch the prawns change colour!

3 Next add the peas and continue to stir-fry for 1 minute. Add the spring onions and remaining sesame oil.

4 Finally, tip in 2 tbsp of water and continue to stir-fry for another 2 minutes. Get out your chopsticks and serve.

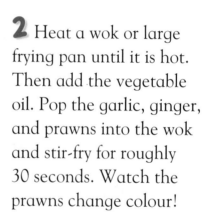
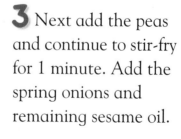
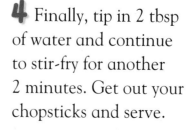

easy to cook. Peas and prawns are lovely colours and a great mix

of textures. Served on a bed of rice, this will

quickly turn into a favourite lunch dish. Good food – fast!

Star tip
For variety, you can use broadbeans or kernels of corn instead of peas.

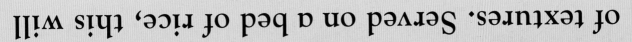

Jamie Oliver

 serves 4

 Preparation: 20 minutes
Cooking: 1 hour 5 minutes

 for the tomato sauce

 splash of olive oil

 ½ leek, roughly chopped

 1 stick of celery, roughly chopped

 1 small courgette, roughly chopped

 ½ red pepper, deseeded, and roughly chopped

 ¼ butternut squash, peeled, deseeded, and roughly chopped

 4 x 400g (14oz) tins Italian plum tomatoes

 sea salt and freshly ground pepper

for the meal

 16 good quality chipolata sausages

 splash of olive oil

 600g (1lb 5oz) jar cooked white beans (haricot, butter bean, or cannellini)

 12 rashers pancetta or streaky bacon

500ml (18 fl oz) tomato sauce (see above)

sea salt and freshly ground pepper

38

Make the tomato sauce

1 Heat a good splash of olive oil in a medium saucepan. Add the leek, celery, courgette, and red pepper, and then cover. Cook for 10 minutes, stirring occasionally, until softened.

2 Next, add the squash and cook with the lid off for 5 minutes, until soft, mushy, and mixed in with the other vegetables.

3 Add the tomatoes, season and bring to the boil. Simmer for 30 minutes, then remove from the heat and blend until smooth. Taste and add more salt and pepper if necessary. Add a splash of water if you find it a little thick.

Star tip This makes 1.7 litres (3 pints) – I often make extra and freeze some for another time.

Make the meal

4 Preheat the oven to 220°C/425°F/gas 7. Put the chipolata sausages into a roasting tin with a little splash of olive oil. Cook in the oven for about 30 minutes, tossing occasionally, until well browned and cooked.

5 Meanwhile, roughly chop four of the pancetta rashers. Heat a large saucepan and add a small splash of olive oil. Gently fry the pancetta until light brown.

6 Drain and rinse the beans then add them and the tomato sauce to the fried pancetta. Simmer gently for 20 minutes and season to taste.

7 Grill the remaining pancetta until crisp. Divide the beans between four plates and top each with four chipolatas and two rashers of crisp pancetta. Serve with crusty bread.

sausages
with
real
baked beans

of healthy veggies without noticing it. It's a great source

these are vital for a healthy mind and body. So eat up!

Antony worrall Thompson

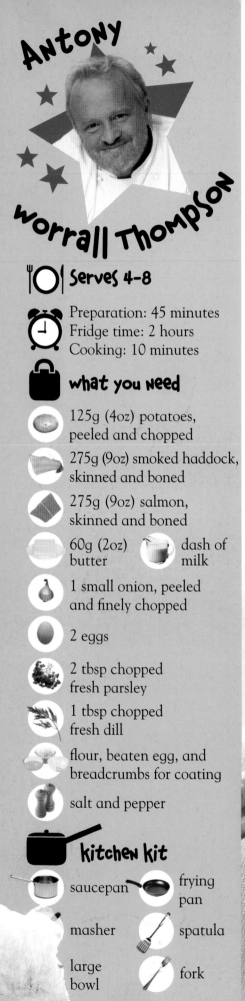

🍴🍽️ Serves 4-8

⏰ Preparation: 45 minutes
Fridge time: 2 hours
Cooking: 10 minutes

what you need

- 125g (4oz) potatoes, peeled and chopped
- 275g (9oz) smoked haddock, skinned and boned
- 275g (9oz) salmon, skinned and boned
- 60g (2oz) butter
- dash of milk
- 1 small onion, peeled and finely chopped
- 2 eggs
- 2 tbsp chopped fresh parsley
- 1 tbsp chopped fresh dill
- flour, beaten egg, and breadcrumbs for coating
- salt and pepper

kitchen kit

- saucepan
- frying pan
- masher
- spatula
- large bowl
- fork

salmon and smoked haddock Fish cakes

Fishcakes are delicious, and ones you have made yourself are even better. Serve with a sea of peas.

How to do it...

1 Boil the potatoes until soft, drain, then mash. Grill the haddock and salmon until flaky and moist. Cool, then flake the fish.

2 Heat half the butter in a pan and cook the onion gently until softened but not brown.

3 Place two eggs into boiling water and boil for 10 minutes. Then put them in cold water to cool. Crack the shell then peel.

4 In a large bowl, use a fork to mix the ingredients – first the flaked fish, potato, and onion, then the eggs, parsley, and dill. Season to taste.

5 Add a dash of milk if the mixture seems too dry, then divide it into 8 patties. Put your fishcakes in the fridge for 2 hours to firm up.

6 Retrieve your fishcakes and coat them in the flour, then the beaten egg, and finally the breadcrumbs.

Star tip

It's fun to make your fishcakes into other shapes too. How about a starfish?

7 Pan-fry the patties in the remaining butter for 5 minutes on each side. Then they're ready to eat!

AntOnY

Worrall Thompson

 Serves 8

 Preparation: 40 minutes
Cooking: 1 hour

 what you need

 450ml (15 fl oz) milk

 1kg (2lb 4oz) white fish fillets

 175g (6oz) cooked and peeled large prawns

 4 tbsp chopped fresh herbs (parsley and chives)

 125g (4oz) unsalted butter

 1 small onion, finely chopped

 175g (6oz) button mushrooms, sliced

 60g (2oz) plain flour

 150ml (5 fl oz) double cream

 half a lemon   salt and pepper

 1kg (2lb 4oz) potatoes, peeled and in chunks

 kitchen kit

 large frying pan   large bowl

 saucepan   sieve

 potato masher   pie dish

Fish pie

Here's a tasty fish pie that will have the kids coming back for more!

Cook the fish...

1 Preheat the oven to 200°C/400°F/gas 6. Place the milk in a frying pan with the fish. Simmer gently for 5 minutes. Remove from the heat and leave to cool.

2 Flake the fish, throwing away any skin and bones. Place in a large bowl with the prawns and herbs.

3 Strain the poaching milk into a jug.

the Jolly Roger

star tip **you can make your pie in one large**

make the sauce...

4 Melt half the butter in a pan and fry the onion until it is soft.

5 Add the mushrooms and cook for a few minutes until tender. Then stir in the flour and cook for a minute, stirring.

6 Remove from the heat and gradually stir in the poaching milk. Season, return to the heat and simmer until thickened, stirring. Stir in half the cream and add a squeeze of lemon.

Finish the pie...

7 Pour the milky mixture into the bowl with the fish and prawns. Mix together and season to taste. Tip into the serving dish and set aside.

8 Boil the potatoes for 15 minutes or until tender. Drain, then mash. Beat in the remaining butter and cream, then season.

9 Carefully spread the mashed potato over the fish mixture. Make wavy line patterns with a fork. Bake for 30 minutes or until bubbling and lightly golden. Serve hot.

Pride of Pie

the Titanic

buttered pie dish, or in little dishes for individual portions.

Ruth Rogers and Rose Gray

 Serves 6

 Preparation: 10 minutes
Cooking: 25 minutes

 what you need

 2 tbsp extra virgin olive oil

 2 garlic cloves, finely sliced

 1 x 400g (14oz) tin tomatoes

 salt and pepper

 1 dried chilli, crushed

 325g (11oz) spaghetti

 100g (3½oz) green beans, topped and tailed

 40g (1½oz) Parmesan cheese, grated

 kitchen kit

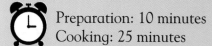 2 large saucepans

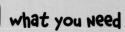 wooden spoon

 colander

Spaghetti with tomatoes and green beans

We are excited by the combination of ingredients in this typical Southern Italian dish – delicious!

Veggies cooked until soft, in a thick

In midsummer you can find incredibly fine green beans from France and Italy...

... these are the best beans to use as they will twirl around the fork with the spaghetti.

...omato sauce... molto bene!

1  Put 1 tbsp olive oil into a heated saucepan. Add the garlic and cook until soft. Mix in the tinned tomatoes, salt and pepper, and chilli, and cook over a medium heat for 20 minutes.

2  'Twist' the spaghetti into a large pan of boiling salted water like in the picture. Cook until soft.

3  Cook the green beans in another pan of boiling water until tender. Drain well. Then tip the beans into the tomato sauce.

4  Drain the spaghetti in a colander then stir it into the tomato and green beans. Season and toss with the remaining 1 tbsp olive oil. Sprinkle with the cheese.

Keith Floyd

Pesto Sauce

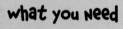 Serves 6

Preparation: 10 minutes

what you need

5 tbsp olive oil

1 garlic clove, quartered

4 tbsp chopped basil, or more if liked

1 tsp salt

4 tbsp chopped parsley

¼ tsp freshly grated nutmeg

30g (1oz) Parmesan cheese, grated

kitchen kit

pestle and mortar

2 Pasta Sauces

These classic pasta sauces make brilliant easy meals. They are especially brilliant if you use only fresh, fresh ingredients. This is not always possible I know, but please try!

Keith Floyd

make the pesto...

Pound 2 tbsp of the oil, the garlic, and basil in a mortar, then gradually beat in the remaining oil. Add the salt, parsley, and nutmeg, and pound until reduced to a paste. Finally stir in the cheese.

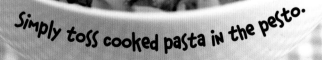
Simply toss cooked pasta in the pesto.

Tomato Sauce

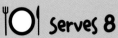 Serves 8

 Preparation: 10 minutes
Cooking: 40 minutes

 what you need

 2 tbsp vegetable oil

 1 onion, chopped

 1 garlic clove, crushed

 2 x 400g (14oz) tins of tomatoes or ripe fresh ones

 150g (5oz) tomato puree

 2 tsp brown sugar

 2 tbsp chopped parsley

 1 tsp chopped oregano

 1 tsp salt

 a pinch of freshly ground black pepper

 1 bay leaf

 kitchen kit

 large saucepan with lid

 wooden spoon

 **star tip** Pasta is great energy food.

make the tomato sauce...

1 Heat the oil in a pan and fry the onion and garlic for 10 minutes, stirring frequently.

2 Add the remaining ingredients: tomato puree, sugar, parsley, oregano, salt, pepper, bay leaf and...

3 ... the tomatoes! Bring to the boil, then reduce the heat, partially cover the pan, and cook for 30 minutes. Remove from the heat, discard the bay leaf, and pour onto some cooked pasta.

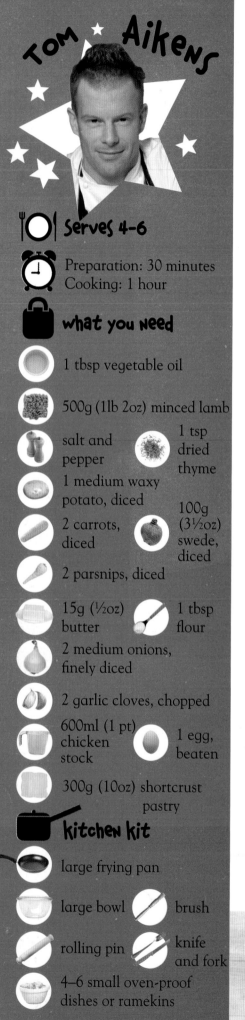

Serves 4-6

Preparation: 30 minutes
Cooking: 1 hour

what you need

1 tbsp vegetable oil

500g (1lb 2oz) minced lamb

salt and pepper

1 tsp dried thyme

1 medium waxy potato, diced

2 carrots, diced

100g (3½oz) swede, diced

2 parsnips, diced

15g (½oz) butter

1 tbsp flour

2 medium onions, finely diced

2 garlic cloves, chopped

600ml (1 pt) chicken stock

1 egg, beaten

300g (10oz) shortcrust pastry

kitchen kit

large frying pan

large bowl

brush

rolling pin

knife and fork

4-6 small oven-proof dishes or ramekins

Pie faces

This is not just another uninteresting lamb dish. It is delicious and simple to make. Plus it is fun to do the pastry part!

star tip

To stick the lid on the pie, glue it on with egg and then fork round the edge.

How to do it...

1 Put the oil in a hot frying pan, and then add the mince, salt and pepper, and thyme. Cook for 5 minutes or until brown.

2 Put the mince in a bowl. Tip the potato into the pan. Cook for 3 minutes. Add the carrots, parsnips, and swede and cook for 5 minutes.

3 Put the cooked vegetables in the bowl with the mince. Add the butter and onions to the pan and cook gently for 3–4 minutes.

4 Add the garlic, then the cooked mince and vegetables to the onion. Stir well, add the flour and cook for one minute.

5 Stir in the stock, a little at a time. Turn up the heat and bring to a boil, then simmer for 10 minutes, stirring occasionally.

6 Roll out the pastry to ½cm (¼in) thick. Cut round a pot to make the lids. Pop the mince mix into the pots, and put on the lids.

7 Roll scraps of pastry into little balls to make faces. Stick onto the pastry lids with egg, then brush with more egg. Bake at 200°C/400°F/gas 6 for 30 minutes, then serve.

49

Antonio Carluccio

 Serves 6

 Preparation: 15 minutes
Rising: 1 hour
Cooking: 25–30 minutes

what you need

 1 tsp dried yeast

 275ml (10 fl oz) lukewarm water

 500g (18oz) strong white bread flour, plus extra for dusting

 2 tbsp olive oil, plus extra for drizzling

 a pinch of salt

 sprinkling of coarse salt

kitchen kit

 2 large bowls

 tea towel

 22 x 30cm (9 x 12in) baking tin

 knife

Focaccia
(italian flatbread)

Your focaccia can be eaten plain or, as they do in Genoa, made into a sandwich. My favourite way to enjoy it is with some gorgeou mortadella cheese whilst it is still warm.

ham

basil

cheese

How to do it...

1 Place the yeast in a bowl with the lukewarm water and wait for the yeast to dissolve.

2 Put the flour in another bowl. Add the oil, yeast liquid, and pinch of salt. Mix together to create a soft, smooth dough.

3 Put the dough on a floured surface and knead for about 10 minutes until it is smooth and elastic.

4 Place the dough in the bowl, cover it with a damp tea towel (or clingfilm), and leave it to rise in a warm place for 1 hour or until it has doubled in size.

5 Preheat the oven to 200°C/400°F/gas 6. Lightly oil a large baking tin.

6 Punch down the dough, then take it out of the bowl and lightly knead it. Press the dough into the baking tin – it should be about 2cm (1in) thick.

7 Brush with olive oil then make small indentations here and there in the dough with your fingertips. Sprinkle the coarse salt over the top.

8 Bake for 25–30 minutes, until a golden-brown crust has formed. As soon as the bread comes out of the oven, drizzle on more olive oil.

9 Remove the bread from the baking tin and leave it to cool on a wire rack. Then cut into squares and serve.

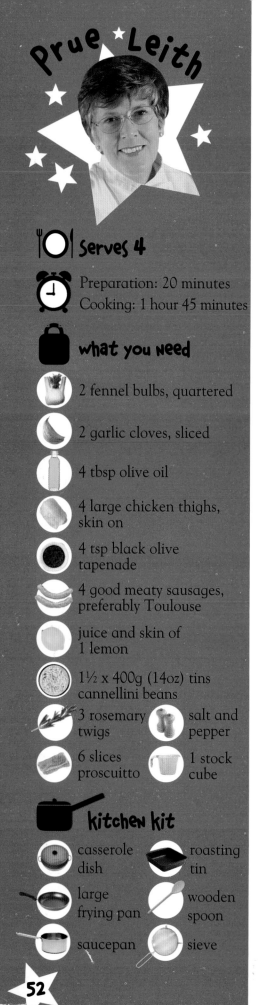

Prue ★Leith

Serves 4

Preparation: 20 minutes
Cooking: 1 hour 45 minutes

what you need

2 fennel bulbs, quartered

2 garlic cloves, sliced

4 tbsp olive oil

4 large chicken thighs, skin on

4 tsp black olive tapenade

4 good meaty sausages, preferably Toulouse

juice and skin of 1 lemon

1½ x 400g (14oz) tins cannellini beans

3 rosemary twigs

salt and pepper

6 slices proscuitto

1 stock cube

kitchen kit

casserole dish

roasting tin

large frying pan

wooden spoon

saucepan

sieve

How to do it...

1 Preheat the oven to 200°C/ 400°F/gas 6. Turn the fennel and garlic in 2 tbsp of the oil. Cook in the oven for 30 minutes.

2 Meanwhile, lift the skin of the chicken thighs and spread a tsp tapenade under each one.

3 Heat the remaining 2 tbsp oil in a large frying pan and brown the chicken thighs well on both sides. Take them out, and then brown the sausages.

4 Layer up the chicken, fennel, and sausages in a casserole dish. Then add the fat from the pan, the lemon juice and skin, the rosemary, salt and pepper. Cover and cook at 220°C/ 425°F/gas 7 for 45 minutes.

5 Drain the liquid from the beans into a saucepan. Add the stock cube and heat until the cube has dissolved.

6 Add the beans and liquid to the chicken, arrange the proscuitto on top and return to the oven, uncovered, for 30 more minutes.

Easy Italian chicken

the grown-ups eat, and this dish is great for a family cook-in.

the chicken and layering up the different bits in the dish.

Star tip

Even olive-haters will think this is delicious!

It is fun squishing the tapenade under the skin of

Puddings and

Heston Blumenthal ⋆ Delia Smith ⋆ Anton Mosiman

Atul Kochhar ⋆ Anton Mosiman

Ainsley Harriott ⋆ Atul Kochhar ⋆ Lesley Waters

Annabel Karmel ⋆ Ross Burden

At the end of a meal, it is a lovely treat to have something sweet. The star chefs have chosen some really delicious recipes. From creative Buzzy bees to medieval Quaking pudding, there is something for everyone, and every occasion.

Cakes

Mary Berry
Phil Vickery

Now for
Something
Sweet

Ainsley Harriott

 makes 12 bars

 Preparation: 20 minutes
Cooking: 35–40 minutes

what you need

- 285g (9½oz) soft butter, plus extra for greasing
- 285g (9½oz) caster sugar
- 285g (9½oz) self-raising flour
- 5 eggs, beaten
- 2 apples, diced
- 60g (2oz) sultanas
- rind and juice of 1 lemon
- a pinch of mixed spice
- a pinch of ground cinnamon
- 60g (2oz) demerara sugar
- 60g (2oz) chopped nuts (optional)

kitchen kit

- large baking tin 28 x 33cm (11 x 13in)
- baking parchment
- wooden spoon
- large bowl
- knife

How to do it...

1 Preheat the oven to 190°C/375°F/gas 5. Grease and line a large baking tin. In a large bowl, mix the butter and caster sugar until lightly creamed.

2 Gradually beat in the flour and eggs until the mixture is smooth. Gently stir in the apples, sultanas, lemon rind, lemon juice, mixed spice, and cinnamon.

Crunchy apple cake bars

3 Pour the mixture into the lined baking tray and spread it out evenly.

4 Then sprinkle the demerara sugar and chopped nuts (optional) over the top. Cook in the oven for 35–40 minutes.

5 Remove from the oven, allow to cool, then cut into bars for a mouth-watering treat.

Star tip when you prepare the fruit, put the lemon juice on the chopped apples to stop them going brown.

Every bite is a satisfying treat.

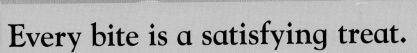

Delia Smith

Chocolate drop MiN

T iny little chocolate bites – soft, light, with

 makes 24

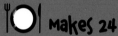 Cooking: 10 minutes

what you need

 5oz (150g) plain flour

 2 level tablespoons cocoa powder

 1 level dessertspoon baking powder

 ¼ teaspoon salt

 1 large egg, lightly beaten

 1½oz (40g) golden caster sugar

 4 fl oz (120ml) milk

 2oz (50g) butter, melted and cooled slightly

 2oz (50g) plain chocolate drops

for the topping

 2¾oz (65g) plain chocolate drops

 24 red glace cherries

 icing sugar, sifted

 You will also need 2 x 12-hole mini-muffin tins, well-greased

Pre-heat the oven to gas mark 6, 400°F (200°C). Start off by sifting the flour, cocoa powder, baking powder and salt into a large bowl.

Then in a separate bowl mix together the egg, sugar, milk and melted butter. Now return the dry ingredients to the sieve and sift them straight on to the egg mixture (this double sifting is essential because there won't be much mixing going on).

What you need now is to take a large spoon and fold the dry ingredients into the wet ones – quickly in about 15 seconds. Don't be tempted to beat or stir, and don't be alarmed by the rather unattractive, uneven appearance of the mixture: this, in fact, is what will ensure the muffins stay light.

58

Once you've mastered the very easy art of making

Muffins with red noses

melted chocolate swirled on the top, on which to fix a whole cherry.

Now fold the chocolate drops into the mixture – again with a minimum of stirring; just a quick folding in.

Divide the mixture between the muffin cups, about 1 heaped teaspoon in each, and bake on a high shelf in the preheated oven for 10 minutes, until well risen.

Then remove the muffins from the oven and cool in the tins for 5 minutes before transferring them to a cooling tray. While they're cooling, place the remaining chocolate drops into a small bowl.

Then place this into a saucepan of barely simmering water without allowing the bowl to touch the water, and allow the chocolate to melt.

Then when the muffins are cool enough to handle, spoon a little melted chocolate on to each one, then place it back on the cooling tray and fix a cherry on top.

If you like, before serving you can give them a dusting of sifted icing sugar.

these, you simply have to make at least 100 – if not more.

HaNSeL aND GReTeL Cake

This gingerbread is a really traditional European cake. It is delicious packed in a picnic, or tucked into your lunchbox for a wholesome snack.

makes 9–12

Preparation: 25 minutes
Cooking: 40–45 minutes

what you need

- 125g (4oz) self-raising flour
- 1 tsp mixed spice
- 3 tsp ground ginger
- 125g (4oz) wholemeal flour
- 40g (1½oz) demerara sugar
- 90g (3oz) sultanas
- 125g (4oz) unsalted butter
- 125g (4oz) each of golden syrup and black treacle
- 1 tsp bicarbonate of soda
- 125ml (4 fl oz) warm milk
- 1 egg, beaten
- 30g (1oz) flaked almonds

kitchen kit

- 15 x 22cm (6 x 9in) baking tin
- greaseproof paper
- sieve
- big bowl
- saucepan

How to do it...

1 Preheat the oven to 180°C/350°F/gas 4. Line the baking tin with greaseproof paper.

2 Sift the self-raising flour, mixed spice, and ginger into a large mixing bowl.

3 Then mix in the wholemeal flour, demerara sugar, and the sultanas.

4 Put the butter, syrup and treacle in a saucepan and heat gently until melted. Add to the dry ingredients and mix everything together.

5 Dissolve the bicarbonate of soda in the warm milk and add the beaten egg. Pour into the flour mixture and beat to form a smooth batter.

6 Pour the batter mixture into the tin and smooth the top.

7 Scatter almonds on top of the batter. Bake in the centre of the oven for 40–45 minutes until well-risen and springy to the touch.

8 Cool slightly in the tin before turning out onto a wire rack. Remove the paper, cut into bars, and serve.

Star tip

Pop the cake bars into an airtight tin the moment they are cool to keep them moist.

Lesley Waters

Serves 9

Preparation: 25 minutes
Cooking: 30 minutes

what you need

125g (4oz) unsalted butter, plus extra for greasing

175g (6oz) caster sugar

2 large eggs, beaten

70g (2½oz) plain flour

40g (1½oz) cocoa powder

1 tsp baking powder

3 tbsp milk

125g (4oz) milk chocolate

125g (4oz) cream cheese

kitchen kit

18cm/7in square cake tin

greaseproof paper

large bowl

electric whisk

wooden spoon

saucepan

sieve

cooling rack

knife

chocolate brownies

Brownies are always a favourite. This cakey version is really chocolatey and has a suprisingly easy-to-make and mouth-watering icing.

Star tip ANOTHER WAY TO MELT CHOCOLATE IS

How to do it...

1 Preheat the oven to 180°C/ 350°F/gas 4. Lightly grease the cake tin with butter and line the base with greaseproof paper.

2 In a bowl, cream together the butter and sugar until pale and fluffy. You can use an electric whisk for this if you have one.

3 Gradually beat the eggs into the butter and sugar mixture.

4 Sift in the flour, cocoa powder, and baking powder and gently fold them in, along with the milk.

5 Spoon the mixture into the tin. Bake in the oven for 30 minutes or until springy to the touch. Allow to cool for 10 minutes, then transfer to a wire rack.

6 While the brownie is cooling, melt the chocolate by breaking it up, popping it in a bowl and melting it over barely simmering water.

7 Let the melted chocolate cool then mix it with the cream cheese. Spread this over the cooled cake then cut into squares to serve.

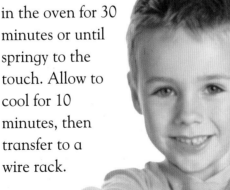

yummy, yummy!

to pop it in the microwave for a minute and then stir.

Makes 12 bees

Preparation: 15 minutes

what you need

4 tbsp smooth peanut butter

1 tbsp honey

2 tbsp dried skimmed milk powder

1 tbsp sesame seeds

1 Weetabix, crushed (could also use shredded wheat)

for decorating

cocoa powder

white chocolate buttons or flaked almonds for the wings

plain chocolate chips for the eyes

kitchen kit

bowl

teaspoon

toothpick

knife

Buzzy bees

How to do it...

1 Mix together the peanut butter and honey, then stir in the milk powder, sesame seeds, and Weetabix.

2 Use your hands to mould the mixture into oval shapes on a teaspoon.

These tasty bees are simple and fun to make and they are just the right size for a healthy snack. Best of all, there is no need to use hot ovens. So get buzzzzzy!

Annabel Karmel

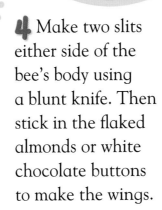

3 Dip a wet toothpick into the cocoa powder and press it onto the bees' bodies to make stripes. You can twirl the toothpick to get more of the brown cocoa powder onto the bee.

4 Make two slits either side of the bee's body using a blunt knife. Then stick in the flaked almonds or white chocolate buttons to make the wings.

5 Make two little hollows using a toothpick and insert chocolate chips for the bee's eyes.

Star tip

The bees can be stored in the fridge for several days.

65

Ross Burden

 serves 6-8

 Preparation: 20 minutes
Cooking: 5 minutes

 what you need

 375g (13oz) icing sugar

 125ml (4 fl oz) milk

 25g (¾oz) butter, plus extra for greasing

 a pinch of salt

 60g (2oz) desiccated coconut

 a few drops of pink or red food colouring

 kitchen kit

 saucepan

 wooden spoon

 small bowl

 baking tin

 knife

 airtight tin

Coconut ice

It's like cooking magic when the mixture turns into crunchy coconut bricks.

MMMMMMM!

This is one of the first things I ever made.

How to do it...

1 Put the icing sugar, milk, butter, and salt in a saucepan. Heat gently, stirring until the sugar dissolves. Then bring to the boil without stirring.

2 Cook the mixture for 5 minutes. It is ready when you drop a little into cold water and it forms a soft ball.

3 Stir in the coconut and allow the mixture to cool off the heat for 10 minutes.

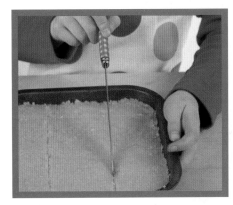

4 Halve the mixture. Colour one half pink, then beat it until it starts to thicken. Beat the white half until it thickens too.

5 Put the white half into a buttered tin and then gently spread the pink half on top. Leave it to set.

6 Cut your coconut ice into squares and serve or keep it in an airtight tin for later.

star tip

If the mixture doesn't fill your tin, it doesn't matter, just fill half of it. The result will be the same.

And I still love it now.

Atul Kochhar

Tandoori phal (Spiced fruit)

 Serves 2

 Preparation: 10 minutes
Marinating: 30 minutes
Cooking: 3–8 minutes

 what you need

 1 red apple, cut into 4, seeds removed

 1 green apple, cut into 4, seeds removed

 ½ mango, cut into 4cm (1½in) slices

 2 slices pineapple

 1 star fruit, cut in 4–6 slices

 for the the marinade

 2 tbsp honey   ¼ tsp black pepper

 3 tbsp yoghurt   1 bay leaf

 1 tsp toasted sesame seeds

 ¼ tsp cardamon powder

 1 tsp lime juice

 kitchen kit

 knife   large bowl

 spoon   skewers

How to do it...

1

First prepare the fruit by chopping it into large chunks.

2

Measure out the ingredients for the marinade and mix them up in a large bowl.

3

Add the fruit chunks and stir them into the marinade. Cover with clingfilm and leave to stand in the fridge for 30 minutes.

4

Thread the fruit onto the skewers so you get each fruit on each skewer. Cook the fruits in a hot tandoor for 3–5 minutes or, alternatively, in a hot oven (220°C/425°F/gas 7) for 6–8 minutes.

This dessert is a great delight – so simple

Serve warm with vanilla ice cream.

to make and versatile. In my experience it is one of the few things that can tempt kids in when they're outside playing – especially with a large dollop of ice cream.

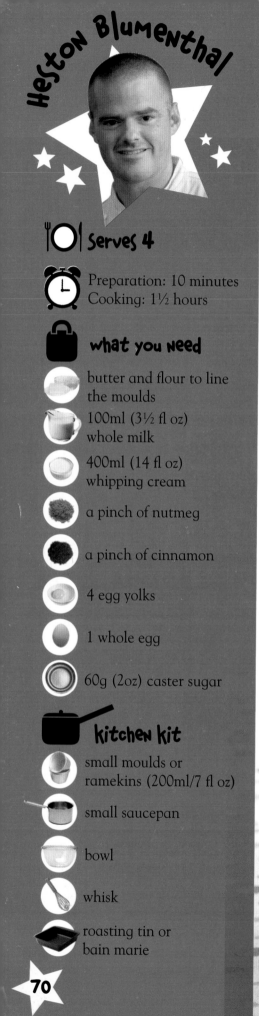

Serves 4

Preparation: 10 minutes
Cooking: 1½ hours

what you need

butter and flour to line the moulds

100ml (3½ fl oz) whole milk

400ml (14 fl oz) whipping cream

a pinch of nutmeg

a pinch of cinnamon

4 egg yolks

1 whole egg

60g (2oz) caster sugar

kitchen kit

small moulds or ramekins (200ml/7 fl oz)

small saucepan

bowl

whisk

roasting tin or bain marie

70

"Quaking" "pudding"

How to do it...

1

Grease the moulds with butter, then tip a tiny bit of flour in and swirl it around until the butter is covered with flour. Tip out excess flour.

2

Warm the milk and cream with the nutmeg and cinnamon in a saucepan over a low heat. Make sure it doesn't boil.

This recipe is really old. Different versions of it were made in medieval times. It is popular in the pub I own – the Hinds Head – and I think it is great fun!

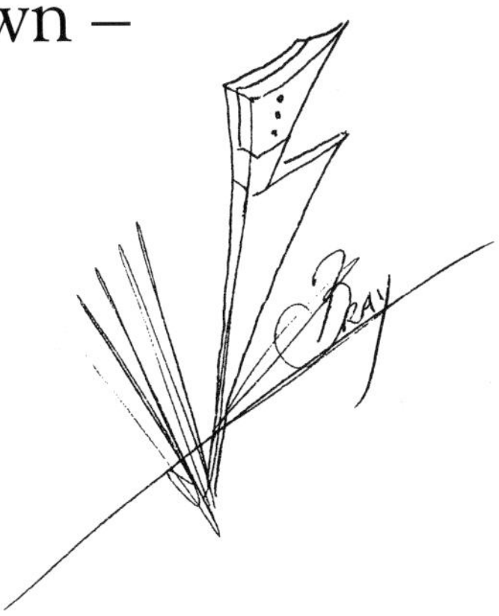

Bray

3

Whisk the egg yolks, whole egg, and sugar in a bowl until combined, but not frothy.

4

Pour the warm milk over the egg and sugar, and stir it all together.

5

Divide the mixture between the moulds, and place them in a roasting tin, or bain marie.

6

Serve with colourful berries and watch them wobble.

Pour cold water into the roasting tin, halfway up the moulds. Cook in a preheated oven at 150°C/300°F/gas 2 for 1½ hours, or until golden brown. Leave to cool, refrigerate, then run a knife around the edge and turn out.

caramel
ice cream

This ice cream has a nice sharp caramel flavour and is as smooth as silk. You will not taste a better caramel ice cream anywhere.

Phil Vickery

 Serves 6

 Preparation: 10 minutes
Cooking: 15 minutes

 for the custard

 250ml (8 fl oz) full cream milk

1 vanilla pod, split

4 medium eggs

60g (2oz) caster sugar

for the Syrup

125g (4oz) caster sugar

70ml (2½ fl oz) cold water

to put it together

275ml (10 fl oz) double cream

¼ tsp salt

 **kitchen kit**

 large saucepan

 whisk

 2 mixing bowls

 sieve

 wooden spoon

 plastic container

How to do it...

1 First you need to make ice cream custard. Put the milk and vanilla pod in a saucepan and bring to the boil.

2 Whisk the eggs and sugar together until fairly pale – don't go mad, there is no need.

3 When the milk is simmering, pour it carefully over the whisked egg and sugar. Whisk well and return to the pan.

4 Cook over a low heat, stirring all the time, until it just starts to thicken. Then remove from the heat, strain through a sieve and leave to cool.

5 Now make the caramel. Put the sugar in a pan and barely cover it with cold water. Stir to dissolve the sugar. Then bring to the boil and cook rapidly until dark brown, but not black. Do not stir.

6 At this point add the cold water and quickly stand well back. The caramel will boil and splutter furiously. Don't panic! Just let it bubble for a minute. Then stir well.

7 Pour the caramel into a bowl to cool. You will end up with a thick caramel syrup.

8 Make sure the custard and caramel are stone cold. Whip the cream into soft peaks, add the salt, then fold in the custard and caramel.

9 Transfer into a pre-chilled container and pop it in the freezer. Make sure you stir it every hour, to churn it, until it solidifies.

 **Star tip** An ice-cream machine will get an even better result. At Step 9, pour the mixture into an ice-cream machine and churn until thick.

Mary Berry

🍴 Serves 4-6

⏰ Preparation: 5 minutes
Cooking: 15 minutes

what you need

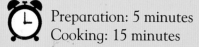

150g (5oz) light muscovado sugar

150g (5oz) golden syrup

60g (2oz) butter

170g (6oz) tin evaporated milk

kitchen kit

large saucepan

wooden spoon

How to do it...

1

Measure out the sugar, golden syrup, and butter and pop it all into a saucepan. Simmer the mixture over a low heat for about 5 minutes, stirring all the time.

2

Then remove the pan from the heat and stir in the evaporated milk.

3

Keep stirring until all the milk has disappeared into the mixture.

4

Put the pan back on the hob and continue to cook for a further 5 minutes or so. It is now ready to serve hot or cold.

Toffee Sauce

I have been making this toffee sauce ever since my children were small and we all adore it.

Mary Berry

Star tip

It keeps in the fridge for a month, but I doubt it will last that long!

perfect as a sauce with many things: ice cream, bananas,

eat this toffee sauce straight out of the pan with nothing.

sponge puddings, and creamy puddings. I can

Thanks to...

Tom Aikens
One of the most exciting young chefs in the UK, Tom is the award-winning owner of the Michelin-starred *Tom Aikens* restaurant in Chelsea, London.

Hugh Fearnley-Whittingstall
Hugh's *River Cottage Cookbook* won the best food book award. He has appeared on *TV Dinners* as well as the *River Cottage* series.

Mary Berry
Mary has published over 60 cookery books, selling over five million copies worldwide. She has been a star guest on TV and radio programmes.

Keith Floyd
Keith Floyd has presented TV cookery programmes for the BBC and Channel 5. He has written 23 books including many bestsellers.

Heston Blumenthal
Heston owns world-famous pubs *The Fat Duck* and *The Hinds Head* in Bray. He is well known for his scientific approach to cooking.

Ainsley Harriott
Ainsley has been a comedian, worked in top hotels, and presented radio and TV shows. He is the host chef on *Ready Steady Cook*.

Ross Burden
Ross is a self-taught cook who won *MasterChef*. He now appears on BBC Two's *Ready Steady Cook* and has published two books.

Ken Hom
Ken has written newspaper articles and bestselling cookbooks and starred in TV series. He is a food and restaurant consultant.

John Burton Race
John rose to fame in *French Leave* and *Coming Home* and published books from both series. He owns restaurants in London and the Home Counties.

Annabel Karmel
Annabel frequently appears on radio and television as the UK's expert on nutritional issues for children. She has written 14 bestselling cook books.

Antonio Carluccio
Antonio owns the successful chain of Carluccio restaurants and food shops. He was host on the popular TV series *Italian Feast*.

Atul Kochhar
Atul was the first Indian chef to win a Michelin star. He worked in top hotels and restaurants before opening his own restaurant, *Benares*.

Prue Leith

A distinguished chef, Prue owns a restaurant and *Leith's School of Food and Wine*. She chairs several charities, including *Focus on Food*.

Ruth Rogers and Rose Gray

Ruth and Rose run the successful *River Café* in London. They have published bestselling cook books and opened a cookery school.

Anton Mosimann

A restaurateur and chef, Anton has worked around the world. He's hosted popular TV series and encouraged the healthy cookery *Cuisine Naturelle*.

Delia Smith

Delia has been teaching the public how to cook for more than 25 years through her successful cookery books and TV work.

Nick Nairn

Nick has written nine successful books and presented a cookery series for the BBC. He owns a restaurant and teaches in a cookery school.

Phil Vickery

Phil is well known for his British food and puddings. He is the author of five books and regularly appears on *Ready Steady Cook* and *This Morning*.

Jean-Christophe Novelli

Jean-Christophe has launched successful restaurants in England and France. In 2005, he helped train budding chefs on ITV's *Hell's Kitchen*.

Marcus Wareing

Voted Restaurateur of the Year at the Tatler Restaurant awards, 2004, Marcus is chef-patron of the Michelin-starred Savoy Grill.

Jamie Oliver

Jamie's fame started with the *Naked Chef* TV series and book. He has sold millions of books and hosted TV series including *School Dinners*.

Lesley Waters

Lesley has worked in TV for over 15 years. She is the author of several cook books and also runs cookery courses for kids.

Gordon Ramsay

Gordon runs restaurants in the famous Connaught and Claridges hotels in London. He starred in *Ramsay's Kitchen Nightmares* and *Hell's Kitchen*.

Antony Worrall Thompson

Antony is one of the most famili and popular TV chefs. He pres *Saturday Feast* and is a regul guest chef on *Ready Steady Cook*.

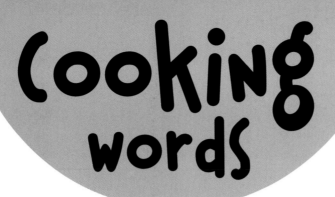

Cooking words

Here are some common cooking words and what they mean. You'll find them in the recipes in this book.

 **Beat** to mix or stir really quickly to break down ingredients or add air and make a mixture smooth

 **Blend** to mix ingredients together using a blender or food processor

 **Boil** to heat a liquid, like water, until it bubbles vigorously and is very hot

 **Chop** to cut into smaller pieces with a knife

 **Cream** to beat butter and sugar together to add air

 **Dice** to chop ingredients into small cubes

 **Drain or Strain** to pour off water from cooked foods or to remove lumps using a sieve or colander

 **Drizzle** to pour slowly, in a trickle

 **Fold** to turn the flat of a metal spoon or spatula round the side of the bowl, then down the middle, turning the mixture gently as you go to keep in air

 **Grate** to rub food against a grater to make small slivers

Grease to rub a small amount of butter over a dish to stop food sticking

Hull to cut or pull out green stalks and leaves from fruit, such as strawberries

Knead

1 Flatten your bread dough slightly, then fold it over towards you.

2 Press the heels of your hands into the dough and push the dough slightly away from you.

3 Turn the dough through ¼ turn, then fold, press and turn again until smooth.

Mash to crush foods, such as potatoes, through the holes in a masher to make them smooth

Melt to heat a solid, such as butter, so it turns to a liquid

Peel to remove the skin of foods such as fruit, vegetables, and eggs

Season to add salt and pepper

Sift to shake a dry, powdery ingredient through a sieve to remove lumps

Simmer to heat a liquid so that it bubbles very gently

Sprinkle to scatter small amounts of an ingredient to make a thin layer

Stir-fry to cook quickly over a high heat in a little oil or fat, stirring constantly

whip to beat ingredients to add air and make them lighter

whisk another word for whip – to add air to a mixture by beating it quickly with a whisk

Index

Acknowledgements

With thanks to:
Pippa Cuthbert and Martha
Dunkerley for additional food styling,
Jane Bull and Mary Ling, Penny Smith
for recipe testing and editorial assistance,
and Carrie Love for editorial assistance.

The publisher would like to thank the
following for their kind permission to
reproduce their photographs and especially
all the chefs who provided photographs
of themselves:

(Key: a-above; b-below/bottom; c-centre;
l-left; r-right; t-top)
Camera Press: Rob Grieg / Time Out 44tl,
77 (Rose & Ruth); Corbis: Cant James /
Sygma 26tl, 76 (Jean); Getty Images: James
Stone 6; Rex Features: 66tl, 76 (Ross); Imre
Diosi 46tl, 76 (Keith); Maggie Hardie 15,
16tl, 76 (Hugh); JEV 70tl, 76 (Heston).

All other images © Dorling Kindersley
For further information see:
www.dkimages.com

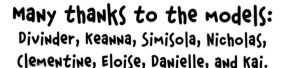

Many thanks to the models:
Divinder, Keanna, Simisola, Nicholas,
Clementine, Eloise, Danielle, and Kai.